YOU HAVE A VOICE

Voting for the Right Candidate

Patie Wool

Copyright 2023 © by Patie Wool

Published by:

PatUch Concepts

patuchconcepts@gmail.com

Year of Publication: 2023

To everyone who understands what it means to exercise their civic right by participating in elections; your vote will count because you have a voice!

Table of Contents

1.

Understanding Your Civic Rights

There comes a time when people must make a decision about who they want in power, to rule over them, for their good cause.

In all areas of life—housing, job, education, etc.—your civil rights are there to defend you from unfair treatment and discrimination.

The laws that safeguard these rights permit specific actions to be taken when they are broken because they form the basis of our democracy. By being aware of your rights, you can spot instances of power abuse and discrimination and receive counsel on how to proceed. One of these rights is the right to choose your leader by way of voting,

Voting is a method that allows a group, such as an electorate or a group, to come together to make a decision or to express an opinion, usually after discussions, debates, or political campaigns. Popular governments use elections to select candidates for important positions. This is a very important subject, especially for continents like Africa.

Residents of a ward who are addressed by a chosen official are known as constituents, and residents who choose to project a voting form for their chosen rival are known as electors.

There are many different methods for gathering votes, however even while many of the navigational methods can also be used as constituent methods, any method that cooks for relative portrayal must be used in decisions.

Voting can take place in a variety of settings in smaller associations. There are polling units, different channels of voting, which will be discussed in subsequent paragraphs.

In a formal setting, using a voting form, people can choose others to work with them, join political organizations with them, or choose positions for them. Casual voting can be done electronically, or it can be done verbally by raising your hand or expressing your agreement.

In a majority rule system, voters decide who will lead the government by casting their ballots in a run for office. This gives voters a chance to select one candidate from among several interesting alternatives. There is little question that contests will be between opposing parties. The two of them will be the most populated and well-known meetings in the nation.

For instance, in some nations, the conservatives and the leftists are at odds. The method by which the person selected addresses people while making decisions in an abnormal majority controls government is by casting a ballot.

The precise opposite of representative democracy is direct majority rules, in which people choose their own delegate to carry out their strategic decisions. A larger part vote occurs when a larger percentage of electors support a comparable candidate or group.

Even while every vote counts, many countries use a variety of factors to determine the winner; it's often not just the famous vote in the aggregate.

For instance, in some countries, the party gaining a majority of the votes cast by the most number of bodies wins, even though they may not have received the most individual votes, they might have lost the well-known vote yet won the seat count.

Many liberal majority rule regimes utilize what is known as a mystery voting form in an effort to prevent people from being touched by others and to protect their political protection.

The purpose of secret ballots is to achieve the most legitimate outcome, with almost no risk of partner pressure, danger, or administrations associated with one's vote: the person decides in support of their genuine preferred selection.

Casting a ballot frequently happens at a surveying station yet casting a ballot should likewise be possible from a distance via mail, or utilizing web casting a ballot or voting. Casting a ballot is deliberate in certain nations, similar to the UK, yet it could be necessary in others, like Australia.

Since nations have various principles about whether casting a ballot is necessary, measurements showing how casting a ballot has changed will contrast. In the event that five marbles are relegated names and are set "on the ballot", and assuming three of them are green, one is red, and one is blue, then a green marble will seldom win the political race.

This is accepting that green marbles structure a variegated gathering of some kind - you wouldn't run three competitors on the off chance that they are no different either way if by some stroke of good luck one can be chosen in any case.

The justification for the green's absence of progress is vote parting. The three green marbles will divide the votes of the individuals who favor green. As a matter of fact, in this similarity, the main way that a green marble is probably going to win is assuming in excess of a little over half of the electors favor green.

Adaptive Frameworks

Assuming the analysis is rehashed with different varieties, the variety that is in the larger part will in any case seldom win. As such, from a simply numerical viewpoint, a single-victor framework will in general lean toward a champ that is unique in relation to the greater part on the off chance that the greater part run various up-and-comers and assuming that the minority bunch runs only one competitor.

With endorsement casting a ballot, electors are urged to decide in favor of however many up-and-comers as they support, so the victor is considerably more liable to be any of the five marbles since individuals who incline toward green will actually want to decide in favor of all of the green marbles.

Experience with the outcomes created by the 'single vote framework' (X-casting a ballot) prompted improvement of the two-round races, or rehash first-past-the-post where the field of up-and-comers is diminished preceding the second round of casting a ballot.

This framework is normal all over the planet. As a rule, the victor should get a larger part of the votes, which is the greater part. In the event that no competitor gets a greater part in the principal round of casting a ballot, the two up-and-comers with the biggest majority run again in the second round of casting a ballot.

Variations exist in regards to these two places: the necessity for being chosen at the main round is once in a while under half, and the principles for support in the overflow might shift.

The outcome that voters seek is a larger administration that will vote for a decision or order of importance that the citizen frequently considers. There are many ways in which citizens and also elected delegates may search to determine what the larger part assessment is.

The three types are the simple, weighted, and association larger part votes. Other multiple-choice methods exist as well, such as the elective vote, endorsement voting, and two-round voting, all of which are also applied in discretionary frameworks.

Appointive Structures

There are several different appointment structures. The parties involved should pick only one person, possibly a panel, or even the entire parliament. Even though the first US electoral system also selected the sprinter as a vice president, there is typically only one winner when electing a president.

Each member of the numerous small voting populace may elect one representative; each member of the smaller number of divided supporters may elect at least two representatives, as in Ireland; or the entire country may be classified as a single region.

2.

History

Elections were employed in ancient Athens, Rome, and to choose popes and Holy Roman emperors, but it was the gradual growth of representative government in Europe and North America starting in the 17th century that gave rise to elections as we know them today.

During that time, the Middle Ages' distinctively holistic theory of representation gave way to a more individualized one that made the person the primary unit of measurement.

The Reform Act

For instance, the British Parliament came to be considered as standing for real people rather than just estates, businesses, and vested interests. How amazing!

Then there was a move to eliminate some people who were seen as rotten or bad eggs that were getting in the way of good governance – a small-population electoral districts run by a single individual or family.

The move or attempt gave birth to the Reform Act. This individualistic view of representation had a direct impact on one of the three significant Reform Acts that increased the size of the electorate in Britain in the 19th century.

The question of precisely who should be included among the governed whose assent was required persisted after governments were accepted as deriving their authority from the consent of the governed and expected to seek that consent on a regular basis.

The implementation of universal adult suffrage was favored by proponents of genuine democracy. By 1920, practically all of western Europe and North America had adult male suffrage; however, women's suffrage was not achieved until slightly later.

Despite the fact that universal suffrage and representative governance are often associated with democracy and despite the fact that competitive elections are one of democracy's features.

A competitive electoral politics does not require universal suffrage. An electorate may be constrained by statutory constraints, as it was before to the enactment of the universal adult suffrage, or it may be constrained by citizens' failure to exercise their right to vote.

Many folks choose not to vote in many nations with open elections. For instance, in Switzerland and the US, less than 50% of voters cast ballots in most elections.

Exclusion, whether legal or self-imposed, can have a significant impact on public policy and even call into question the legitimacy of a government, but it does not impede elective decision-making as long as voters are presented with real options.

Aristocracy

During the 18th century, participation in politics was mostly contingent on belonging to an aristocratic movement. Local customs and arrangements primarily governed election participation.

Although the American and French revolutions established nominal equality between all citizens, the vote remained a tool of political power held by a very small number of people.

Three consecutive periods saw the introduction of competitive elections based on universal suffrage in sub-Saharan Africa.

Following decolonization, several nations had elections in the 1950s and 1960s.

There were exceptions despite the fact that the majority of them returned to authoritarian regimes. After certain military dictatorships were overthrown (such as those in Ghana and Nigeria) and other countries in Southern Africa underwent decolonization in the late 1970s, elections were implemented in a smaller number of nations.

More than a dozen African nations, including Benin, Mali, South Africa, and Zambia, saw democracy and competitive elections beginning in the early 1990s as a result of the end of the Cold War and the cessation of military and economic help from Western nations.

3.

Choosing the Candidate to Vote for

This is one of the most important parts of an electoral process. I had established earlier that it is your right as an adult who is a citizen of a country, to be involved in the electoral process by voting a candidate of your choice. How do you go about this? There are certain things to look out for.

The first thing is to be the judge; yes, be the judge. Analyze your prospects' stances on many topics, as well as their potential for leadership and experience in the workplace. Both are crucial. Decide which topics are important to you and what traits you are looking for in a leader as your first step.

When you think about topics, examine the concerns that you want the government to handle on a local, state, and federal level. Think about the traits that a good leader might possess while considering leadership attributes. Do you search for qualities like intelligence, honesty, and communication skills? Then what?

There's more you can do, look through the pictures — In campaign materials, slogans, brand awareness, and personality are frequently the only things that stand out. Over reliance on the media and the accelerated pace of life have significantly altered how consume political news is consumed. Today's campaigns prioritize style far more than substance.

In today's politics, an image campaign is frequently used. It takes time and effort to look for problems when images have taken over the political arena. But, you will have a margin of assurance that you will receive the facts you require in order to vote confidently as your reward.

Campaign Details

Collect information about the candidate from a number of sources, including their websites, social media accounts, speeches, radio and television commercials, literature, debates, and more. Verify the fliers and posters.

That brochure that was tucked under your door or given to you at the store can be filled with shallow images, or it might even contain lies, misrepresentations, or evasions. Critically review it. Does it reveal more about the candidate's commitment to their family than it does about their qualifications or positions on issues?

Watch out for allegations or other remarks made about rivals, especially if they are made so close to election day that they cannot be refuted or refuted.

Nowadays, almost all candidates have websites, and a large number of them use social media sites like Facebook and Twitter. You want to discover the most comprehensive list of positions on these websites because these are the most direct methods of interacting with voters looking for information.

Seeing that this is information that the candidates have provided, think of it as their primary marketing pitch. Is the message one of good or bad? Does the candidate offer voters a chance to assess their education and work history?

Are there justifications for a candidate's stance on a particular issue? Is the content accurate and fact-based? Websites are frequently updated as campaigns move along, so the amount of content may eventually rise.

Like I said earlier, you are first the judge because your votes count.

Consider a candidate's arguments and appeals; these are emotional appeals. then determine if they are only directed at your emotions. Is the candidate attempting to enrage you to the point that you will accept certain claims at face value?

Maybe you should feel sorry for someone who grew up in poverty, but you shouldn't vote for them. Check the facts. Avoid being influenced or distracted by political hyperbole. Recognize manipulative tactics and avoid them.

You can examine candidates' social media accounts throughout time to observe how they respond to recent events because candidates will undoubtedly publish their opinions on current events. Ask yourself some questions whenever you see or hear a paid political advertisement.

What did the advertisement reveal about the candidate? Have you discovered anything regarding problems or requirements? Or was the advertisement made solely to influence how viewers felt or acted toward the candidate?

How significant were the screenplay, the setting, and the music? Was the advertisement intended to target women, minorities, elderly voters, or certain interest groups? If the candidate wants you to or if you can separate the glitter from the substance, you can learn about issues even from a 60-second TV or radio commercial.

Commitments

There are commitments that an elective official can keep and issues that cannot be resolved through politics. Realistic goals can be achieved by public authorities, but neither voters nor candidates should have unrealistic expectations.

Think about how feasible those promises are when all you hear are promises, promises. Look into the matters that are significant to you. Choose the changes you believe your neighborhood, state, and nation most need. What do you wish to remain unchanged? Which of your interests is each candidate's proposed program serving?

Think about and consider your options. Pay attention to those on all sides of the argument. Check out the causes and effects. Think about the trade-offs necessary to achieve your goals.

Be on the lookout for insinuation or unsupported claims; they are common. In a political campaign, keep an eye out for quotes. If voters are naive, murky signals can impact an election long before a fair-campaign probe or a slander lawsuit can put an end to them.

The ambiguous query has the same impact. It is simple to misrepresent the truth when someone asks, "Where was my opponent when the chips were down about expanding employment insurance?" without revealing that the issue was never brought up for a vote.

A lot of candidates put a lot of effort into avoiding responding directly to queries. And any candidate who claims to have a clever, simple solution to a challenging issue is simply feigning ignorance. Be wary of candidates that just discuss advantages without addressing costs or the specifics of how a program would operate.

4.

Assessment of the Candidates

Keep a journal as you study the materials you have gathered and note the candidates' positions on your top concerns. Do the materials present a comprehensive picture of the candidates to you? What particular inferences can you make about their positions on various issues?

Next, I will point out areas that require assessment.

1. Capability to lead

It's challenging to judge whether a candidate will make a good leader. How can you tell if a candidate for government will be trustworthy, forthright, and able to function under duress?

2. Argument

Because you are so prepared to comprehend the questions and answers and assess the competitors' performance, you should enjoy watching a televised debate. Learn about the debate sponsor before the event and keep track of any disputes regarding the debate itself.

A good format should be informative about the candidates and the issues, fair and engaging, and it should enable you to assess the candidates' leadership potential.

Does it keep your attention? Does it allow the candidates' differences to come to light? Does it make it simple for candidates to debate concerns and answer critics? You should give these important factors serious consideration.

3. Experience and background

How ready are they for the position? See how the candidates behave. Do they agree to give speeches or take part in debates in front of various groups, including some who might not be sympathetic? Find out as much as you can about the candidates' personalities by attentively reading the campaign literature. Are concerns or just image highlighted? Are they true?

Moreover, ask people in your town who follow political campaigns for their thoughts. Find out who they support and why by speaking with three people (who are not family). Find out what has influenced their thinking. Was it a plan or proposal that the candidate had suggested? A certain topic or group that they have strong feelings about?

Find out how the candidates are financing their campaigns. Do they raise money from their own pockets, from a select group of affluent donors, from a large number of small donations, or from political action committees?

The media must report on a variety of facts on campaign contributions that must be provided to the government. What potential effects might these gifts have on the candidate's performance in office?

At the conclusion, give your applicants a grade for their comments and the visuals they presented. They might be strong. It is obvious that the influence of visuals can influence voters to ignore what is being spoken.

Are the candidates' ages, sexes, appearances, or other physical traits influencing your decision? Who gave off a more comfortable, truthful, and assured vibe? Who, for instance, makes better use of television by gazing at you directly?

Determine who replies or avoids the questions while evaluating substance. Do the candidates express where they stand on the issues, or do they instead use emotive language or catchphrases? Is it personal or aimed at the other candidate's policies if someone criticizes their rival? Do the candidates seem knowledgeable and do their responses reflect their prior positions?

Evaluate the data you have gathered, evaluate the candidate you have chosen, and support the candidate you believe in. You can offer to work on a campaign in your free time.

On election day, cast your vote!

5.

Election Questions And Answers

---

1. Why should election day should be declared a national holiday?

It is a step toward encouraging a large number of people to vote by turning out in large numbers.

2. Why is voting significant?

Elections give citizens the opportunity to choose their leaders and hold them responsible for their actions while in government.

3. How trustworthy are internet polls? In practice, according to pioneers of science based polling data, their findings are no less trustworthy than those of conventional polls. They also claim that the issues with conventional polling, such as insufficient data for quota design and low response rates for phone polls, can contribute to systemic bias.

4. Is voting for oneself in elections is possible? Yes it is